A Reflective Devotional

Untangled Advent

Finding Hope in a Weary World

Megan B. Nilsen

Farmhouse
Publishings

Farmhouse Publishings, LLC,
P.O. Box 333
Spearfish, SD 57783

ISBN: 979-8-9906020-9-0

Design by Heidi Caperton

Printed in the United States of America

To my Christmas — loving husband, who believes there's no such thing as listening to Christmas music too early in the year or watching Christmas movies too many times! *Bless his heart.*

Table of Contents

Weary: adjective

physically or mentally exhausted by hard work, exertion, strain, etc.;
fatigued; tired: *weary eyes; a weary brain*
Synonyms: worn-out, spent[1]

"Seeing that a Pilot steers the ship in which we sail, who will never allow us to perish even in the midst of shipwrecks, there is no reason why our minds should be overwhelmed with fear and overcome with weariness."[2]

// John Calvin

"God gives God. That is the gift God always ultimately gives. Because nothing is greater and we have no greater need, God gives God. God gives God, and we only need to slow long enough to unwrap the greatest Gift with our time: time in His Word, time in His presence, time at His feet."[3]

// Ann Voskamp

"Come to me, all of you who are weary and burdened,
and I will give you rest" (Matthew 11:28 CSB).

// Jesus

1   Dictionary.com | Meanings & Definitions of English Words. (2021). In Dictionary.com. https://www.dictionary.com/browse/weary

2   *A quote by John Calvin.* (n.d.). https://www.goodreads.com/quotes/196943-seeing-that-a-pilot-steers-the-ship-in-which-we

3   Voskamp, A. (2013). T*he Greatest Gift: Unwrapping the Full Love Story of Christmas.* Tyndale House Publishers, Inc.

Introduction

*L*adies and Gentlemen, *Drumroll please...*

Welcome to the ever—hopeful, often—exhausting, frequently frenetic annual holiday season! May the odds be ever in your favor.

Alright, that greeting might be a bit much, but there's always something *extra* in the air this time of year, isn't there?

Not only does the weather shift in many parts of the world, but so does the music, the store decorations, and, of course, the overpriced, seasonal latte choices. Are you team pumpkin spice or peppermint mocha?

Marketers everywhere capitalize on the idea that the best place you could ever find yourself would be *"home for the holidays..."*

This phrase often conjures images of pajamas—clad children scampering down Grandma's creaky staircase before dawn while Mom and Dad stumble down bleary-eyed and reach for much—needed caffeine. The cozy home's exterior boasts a silent orchestra of fresh falling snow while the interior stokes every heart with a crackling fire and Bing Crosby crooning in the background.

Warm and fuzzy, indeed.

However, these magical images are often far from reality in a world where peace on earth exists only in sappy, staged movies (or because a harried mom has done cartwheels, backflips, and double layouts to try and curate the "perfect" day only to realize the turkey is burned, the new clothes don't fit, and the kids would rather be with their friends).

The holiday season can also sting on a personal level as we grieve lost loved ones or gear up to experience familiar pressure cooker family dynamics that feel more "dys" than "functional."

One Christmas season stands out for me personally, among all others to date, as the height of stress and chaos.

In December 2011, just three weeks before Christmas, our family finalized the international adoption of our two youngest children. As a newly formed family of six, we boarded a red-eye flight from Addis Ababa, bound for Colorado Springs. The phrase "home for the holidays" no longer felt like a marketing tagline; it would be a reality!

We would be home for Christmas! What a wonderful gift indeed.

As expected, text messages streamed in from friends and family excited to meet our new crew. I just didn't realize that, as eyelids drooped while the wheels of the Lufthansa jumbo jet lifted off the runway, we were effectively stepping through the looking glass and tumbling head-first down the rabbit hole of transition and grief.

Imagine two wide-eyed Ethiopian siblings (ages 7 & 5 at the time) traveling around the globe, emerging dazed and confused on a frosty December night. The kids shivered as they rolled their bags through the parking lot in the foreign, frozen tundra of Colorado. The atmosphere of shock and awe cranked up like the heat in our car as we headed home.

Lest I deceive you into thinking this story had an immediate fairy–tale ending, I assure you the transition home was nothing short of "other-worldly" for the lot of us. Grief loomed large over our house for quite a while, manifesting in all sorts of tantrums and tears. And not only from the kids! I confess my own heart also wrestled to embrace the new family dynamics. Christmas Day was more of a chaotic circus than a serene, silent night.

"Weariness" was most definitely the word of the year.

As I write this, I gratefully testify that God's grace and mercy have brought immense healing and attachment within our family, but the memory resurfaces each time December rolls around.

I'm not sure what's overwhelming you right now, but even if you're in relatively smooth waters, the holiday season can barrel down like a fierce nor'easter.

The heart rate monitor on your smartwatch is likely climbing as your eyes glance at the date on the calendar. Your mind will immediately track your mounting to-do list like a bloodhound in order to position you for the main events.

On your mark, get set... Commence the craziness!

The planning. The cooking. The cleaning. The shopping. The decorating. The wrapping. The parties and performances.

There's a good chance you could get so caught up in all the exhausting DOING that you thwart any possibility of experiencing the life-giving BEING. *(Ask me how I know.)*

Taking time to sit with this devotional and rest in the presence of God this holiday season is a fantastic first step to righting the ship and heading in a direction that promises God's love and peace instead of chaos and exhaustion.

Accessing the incredible presence of our coming King in the midst of the world's unique brand of Christmas craziness will fortify you to not only do what you *need* to do but also give you the Holy Spirit strength necessary to resist the very real temptation of being distracted by *everything else.*

Meandering through the pages of this devotional will allow you to hang out in a passage of Scripture so rich with gospel grace that even if you've read this story a hundred times, there will no doubt be a new revelation waiting for you on the other side. As you commit your heart to meeting with Jesus, the be-still-and-know life is not only accessible to you in the midst of the hustle but promises deep hope and transformation for your very soul.

This is your holy invitation to put first things first and help your heart find its true home. This is your opportunity to lay down your burdens and lean into the God-with-us

presence of Jesus. As a result, all lesser things will fall dutifully in line or by the wayside entirely.

As you shed the scales of shoulds and oughts, your soul will find a holy pace and much-needed space to exchange exhaustion for rest and stress for solace in Jesus.

Sounds incredible, doesn't it?

I created this for you because this is exactly what my soul needs on a regular basis as well. There is a Light that pierces through all darkness.

And His name is Jesus.

When His light illuminates and dissipates the darkness that casts a shadow on your heart, you have the distinct possibility of being "home" all year round.

That is good news indeed!

Where Are We Headed?

This devotional focuses on the first glimpse we have of the Light of God coming into the natural world in human form by way of a faithful young woman (and unsuspecting soon-to-be mother) named Mary.

Her story has always captured my heart because I see within it a very real picture of what life with God often looks like. This girl's just planning her wedding to the love of her life, likely checking off items from a never-ending to-do list, when all of a sudden, an angel appears with a startling message about how God has found favor with her and has some wild plans to partner with her to save His wayward people.

Naturally, she's dazed, confused, and all tangled up, trying to make sense of what's happening. Talk about disconcerting! I would absolutely start firing away a litany of questions. You know, make God give me some reasonable details.

But Mary doesn't do that. She doesn't push back. Instead of reacting in knotted-up bewilderment, she displays incredible, surrendered faith. She yields herself, body and soul, to the will of God.

I get the Holy Spirit chills every time I think of this. What could it mean for you and me to yield ourselves to the work of the Spirit like Mary did, every day, of every year? And not just at Christmastime.

Diving into the pages of Mary's story is an invitation to encounter God in the midst of the everyday, tangled-up human life. A chance to bring your doubts, concerns, troubles, and worries to the feet of Jesus.

This is an opportunity to lay it all before God and ask Him to shine His Light in dark places. To take weariness and worry and ask Him to faithfully exchange them for eternal love, hope, life, and peace—once again.

Now What? The Nuts and Bolts of this Study.

We'll slow down the pace and marinate in a couple of beautiful passages of Scripture that I've broken down into *five different Acts* to guide you toward encounter and reflection on your faith journey:

Act One: *The Beginning // John 1:1–18*

Act Two: *The Becoming // Luke 1:26–33*

Act Three: *The Believing // Luke 1:34–38*

Act Four: *The Blessing // Luke 1:39–45*

Act Five: *The Rejoicing // Luke 1:46–56*

Each *Act* will direct you along the following steps:

- **LISTEN + LOG**: Listen to the correlating **teaching episode*** recorded on the **Kingdom Life Coaching podcast**. A QR code is available at the start of each Act for you to link and listen on Apple podcasts or Spotify. If you do not have access to either of these apps, don't worry. This podcast is available on multiple platforms. All you need to do is look up "Kingdom Life Coaching" (with Megan Nilsen) and search for that specific episode number. *(*This study was originally titled "O Weary World, Rejoice" so you may hear me refer to that title throughout the teaching episodes, but the meat of the teaching directly connects to this updated devotional!)*

  I **recommend listening** to the podcast when you **can sit down with pen in hand and take note** of anything the Holy Spirit specifically highlights to you because His voice is accessible at all times! There is a section for you to **log your aha moments**—which are often the most powerful. However, I understand life isn't always conducive to adding larger chunks of silence and solitude for copious note-taking (especially over the holidays)—so absorb what you can! You can listen in a big, comfy living room chair, in your car, or on a walk. Make plans to *do whatever you can, and God will meet you there.*

- **RECOGNIZE**: It's important to **connect with your inner world** and pay attention to what you're feeling at any given moment. God invites you to cast all your anxieties on Him because He cares for you (1 Peter 5:7 NLT). This brief section allows you the opportunity to **recognize what's got you tangled up** at the moment. You no longer need to carry these stressors alone.

- **RENEW:** You'll have the opportunity to take a moment before you dive into the intentional exploration sections to **renew your thoughts**. To breathe deeply and **praise God for the good gifts** He has given you in the midst of weary times.

- **EXPLORE:** This section will **guide you through a series of Scripture readings**. You will **start with the key passage** of that section and move into **related passages** that enhance each *Act's* particular theme. Take your time going through the Scripture verses and make note of anything the Holy Spirit highlights to you as interesting or relevant for personal exploration.

- **ASK:** You will finish each *Act* by navigating a series of **journaling questions**. These questions are meant to usher you into a space of deep **reflection and introspection** for spiritual growth and transformation. This is your invitation to get super real. It's tempting to skip this piece when you don't have time or energy to mine for your truest response, but if you can slow your brain and travel deeper inside your soul, the more revelation, breakthrough, joy, hope, and peace you will experience!

There is **no prescriptive time-frame** for completing this devotional study.

It was originally written with the intention of the reader going through each *Act* in a five or six day time period, but you may parse it out however you like, depending on the time you have available for deeper study and preferred pacing.

Simply start whenever you have this book in hand and end whenever the Lord directs.

And guess what—you don't even have to finish this before Christmas day! *(I know, right??)* God's Word is alive and active, relevant in and out of every season, including the holidays. *Wink.* I think it's incredibly powerful to study and reflect on the birth of Jesus during Advent—the time of year in which we celebrate this incredible, life-changing gift of grace—but don't let the calendar hem you in.

Take all the time you need to thoughtfully savor Christ's presence in the midst of His Word and receive everything the Father has for you - no matter the date or time. Even spending five-minute chunks in His powerful presence can bear much fruit!

There are blank pages at the end of each *Act* and in the back of the book for you to **log anything extra** that feels particularly important, such as prayers, thoughts, questions, Holy Spirit promptings, and free-flow musings. If there is one thing I know for sure—it's that our God is a God of continual surprises—just ask Mary! You may have some extra gifts coming your way, and you definitely don't want to miss them.

Oh!! One more thing!

I have curated a **fantastic worship playlist** to accompany this study. These songs position my heart to experience Jesus profoundly each Christmas, and I want to pass them along to you. Music often heals the wounds our soul experiences and creates a language

that connects us to the Kingdom of Heaven in a way nothing else can. Use this QR code to find the playlist on Spotify and allow the moving music of the season to fill your heart and your home.

Praying for you as you begin this journey,

Megan

PS – If the calendar does flip and January 1st finds you reflective and anticipating God's hand at work in your life for the coming year, you can access a brief but powerful New Year reflection journal to mine for some extra revelation and vision for the new year by going to newyearreflections.com

(You can also access the corresponding Kingdom Life Coaching podcast episode available for additional explanation and teaching: Episode 42, 6 Reflection Questions to Start the New Year with Intentional Faith.)

Act One

The Beginning
John 1:1-18

"In the **beginning** was the Word, and the Word was with God, and the Word was God. He was with God in the **beginning**. All things were created through him, and apart from him not one thing was created that has been created. In him was life, and that life was the light of men. That light shines in the darkness, and yet the darkness did not overcome it."

(John 1:1-5 CSB)

Let's Get Started...

LISTEN

Listen to **Episode 37** of the **Kingdom Life Coaching Podcast** // *Untangled Advent* // *Act One* // *The Beginning*. (Main teaching begins around minute 6:00.)

Spotify

Apple

LOG

Jot down anything the Holy Spirit highlights to you throughout the teaching in this episode.

_____

_____

_____

RECOGNIZE

Pay attention to what you're feeling. This brief section allows you the opportunity to **recognize what's got you tangled up** at the moment and give your concerns to God.

Write down a couple of specific things you'd like God to carry:

_____

_____

_____

_____

_____

RENEW

Cultivating an awareness of God's goodness is an excellent remedy for weariness. Identify three things you are grateful for today:

1.

2.

3.

Before reading the Scripture and journaling questions, take a deep breath. Relax your heart and mind. Ask the Holy Spirit to meet you and speak to you throughout this study. Prepare yourself to hear from Him.

EXPLORE

Read the key Scripture passage for *Act One* // **John 1:1-18**

- It is not tough to make the argument that we live in a very dark world. Looks like things have always been this way. What does John tell us about the Light of Jesus in **John 1:5**? Write this verse below. How does this truth shape your perspective in the midst of darkness?

- What two things does John say about the world's "acceptance" of Jesus in **John 1:10-11**?

- What truth does John reveal about our place in the story in **John 1:12-13**?

- The law was given through Moses. According to **John 1:17,** what came through Jesus Christ?

Related Scripture Readings for Further Exploration

What do you continue to learn about Jesus' existence as part of the Trinity in the following passages?

Genesis 1:1-5 - What (who) hovered over the waters in the very beginning of the creation of the world?

John 7:28-29 - What did Jesus say to those listening in the temple about who He is and where He came from?

John 17:1-5 - How long have Jesus and the Father shared in glory together?

Colossians 1:15-1 7 - How long has Christ existed? How is He described, and what did He create?

ASK:

The following questions invite you to go deeper with Jesus and ask the Holy Spirit to help you access the innermost parts of your soul. It's tempting to skip certain questions when you don't have an immediate response. That's okay. If your mind is blank, just ponder these things in your heart like Mary did. This is your personal experience. Ask God to give you the Holy Spirit revelation and come back to answer more thoroughly at a later time.

- What does it mean to you to know Jesus has always existed? How does this truth shape your faith as we prepare to celebrate his birth here on earth?

- The Apostle John (Gospel author) makes it clear John the Baptist (forerunner) was not "the light." His job was to point the way to the true Light, Jesus, the Messiah. In what specific ways does your life point to the Light of Jesus to those around you? What roles do you inhabit that lead/bless others?

- Take a moment to think of the people in your life and sphere of influence. Ask God to highlight someone specific you can love in an extra special way right now. Write down the name (or names if there are multiple!) and some practical ways to show them God's love that would bless them in this season.

- In **John 1:12**, we read that all who receive Jesus as Savior and Lord have the right to become children of God. What does this mean for you specifically? How would you describe what a child of God looks like?

- In the Old Testament, God revealed Himself through various people and prophets. His Spirit hovered in certain times and spaces and on specific people. But all that changed through the birth, death, and resurrection of Jesus Christ! **Re-read John 1:14**. Write a prayer expressing your response to this world-altering truth. What do you want to say to the Father, and how do you desire to prepare your heart for this season with Jesus?

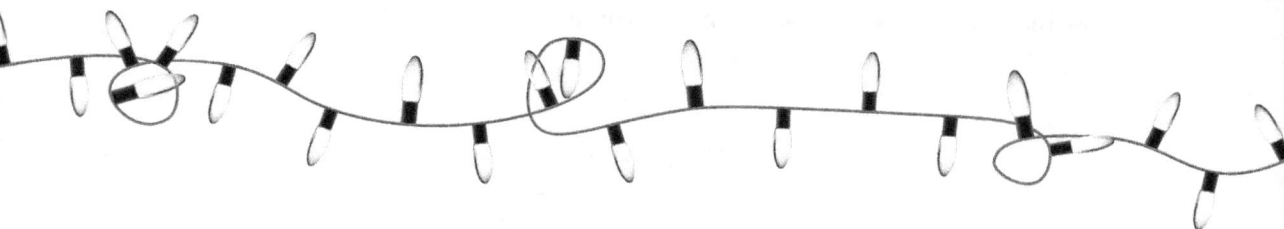

Reflective Closing Prayer

Dear Lord, Thank you for making all things - from the beginning of time until now. You are the Creator God and I worship only you! You are the true source of all life and hope; may my heart never seek it elsewhere. You are the Light that shines in every part of my life. Even in the darkest times, I trust you are constantly working all things for my good because you care for me.

Extra Space for Holy Spirit downloads and musings—use this space to journal and pray over anything God brings to your awareness.

Act Two

The Becoming

"During the sixth month of Elizabeth's pregnancy, the angel Gabriel was sent from God's presence to an unmarried girl named Mary, living in Nazareth, a village in Galilee. She was engaged to a man named Joseph, a true descendant of King David. Gabriel appeared to her and said, 'Rejoice, beloved young woman, for the Lord is with you and you are anointed with great favor.'

Mary was deeply troubled over the words of the angel and bewildered over what this may mean for her. But the angel reassured her, saying, 'Do not yield to your fear, Mary, for the Lord has found delight in you and has chosen to surprise you with a wonderful gift. You will **become** pregnant with a baby boy, and you are to name him Jesus. He will be supreme and will be known as the Son of the Highest. And the Lord God will enthrone him as King on the throne of his ancestor David. He will reign as King of Israel forever, and his reign will have no limit."

(Luke 1: 26-33 TPT)

Take the next step...

LISTEN

Listen to **Episode 38** of the **Kingdom Life Coaching Podcast** *// Untangled Advent // Act Two // The Becoming.*

Spotify

Apple

LOG

Jot down anything the Holy Spirit highlights to you throughout the teaching in this episode.

_____

_____

_____

RECOGNIZE

Pay attention to what you're feeling. This brief section allows you the opportunity to **recognize what you are worried about** at the moment and give your concerns to God.

Write down a couple of specific things you'd like God to carry:

_____

_____

_____

_____

_____

RENEW

Cultivating an awareness of God's goodness is an excellent remedy for weariness. Identify three things you are grateful for today:

1.

2.

3.

Before you start reading the Scripture and journal questions, take a deep breath. Relax your heart and mind. Ask the Holy Spirit to meet you and speak to you throughout this study. Prepare yourself to hear from Him.

EXPLORE

Read the key Scripture passage for *Act Two //* **Luke 1:26-33**

- Why do you think this section is called "the becoming?" What did becoming mean for Mary?

- What was Mary's immediate response to the angel Gabriel's pronouncement?

- What did Gabriel say back to her?

- What prophecy did Gabriel reveal about this soon-to-be-born Son?

Related Scripture Readings for Further Exploration

What do you learn about the angel Gabriel and his other divine assignments?

Luke 1:6-29 - Which angel appears? Note the differences between Zechariah's and Mary's experiences. Why do you think it happened this way?

Daniel 8:15-19 - Which angel appears to Daniel? What is his purpose in coming?

Matthew 1:18-23 - Who appears to Joseph? What does he say, and why was his appearance so important?

ASK:

The following questions invite you to go deeper with Jesus and ask the Holy Spirit to help you access the innermost parts of your soul. Take some time to journal your heartfelt answers.

- The angel Gabriel told Mary she would *become* pregnant. The word "become" literally means *"to come into being, change, grow to be."*[4] Write down one way in which you have changed over the years—for the better! Testify of God's faithfulness regarding your development in that space.

- Now, imagine your future self. Is there an area of growth for you? In what specific way do you desire to become more like Christ? Ask God to show you His plans for you in that area.

---

4   becoming. (n.d.). In Merriam-Webster Dictionary. https://www.merriam-webster.com/dictionary/becoming

- Is there something you have been praying about for a long time? So long you are potentially weary of the 'same old' prayer? Before you give up in exasperation, give it one more go. You are in good company with Hannah, Anna, and the Persistent Widow. Lay your burden down on this page and ask God to give you His Kingdom perspective. Listen for His voice. What does He want you to know about this circumstance right now?

- Mary was given a seemingly impossible task. Is there something specific you sense the Lord calling you into about which you think, *"No way! I am not the person for that job."* Write out what you feel God is inviting you to do. In what ways are you tempted to see yourself as "unusable" to God?

- Now, apply a Kingdom lens and ask God to speak into this situation. What is His response to your hesitation? How might He be rebuilding your faith to remind you that He partners with the most "unlikely" for His Kingdom purposes?

- We see in Matthew 1:18-23 that God provided a partner for Mary. She would not be alone! Who has God paired you with on your faith journey? Write down any names that come to mind. Thank God for them, and consider writing each one a note of encouragement. Express the blessing they are in your life and how they have shaped your faith to help you become who you are today!

- When angels appear in Scripture, they seem to always say, "Do not be afraid." Why do you think that is? What are you afraid of right now? Ask God to tell you His truth about that situation. Write down a specific exchange you can make for the fear you so easily experience. What is God offering you instead?

- How can you live expectant of a new thing right now? Prophesy and declare what God is doing in your life. Write down whatever He reveals to you and the next right step of faith to take in that area.

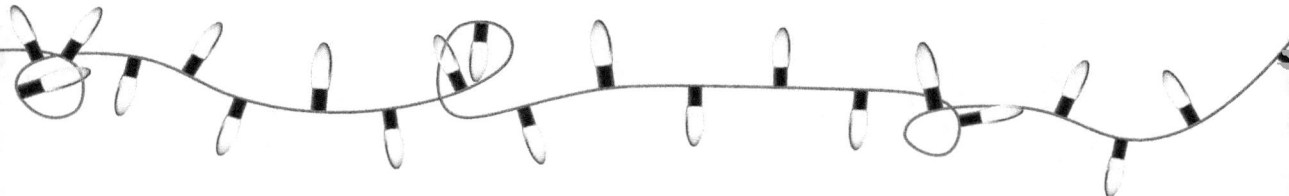

Reflective Closing Prayer

Dear Lord, I admit I sometimes feel afraid in this dark and weary world. And yet your Light of redemption is always shining and lighting the way for those who love you! Thank you for sending messages of hope to remind me that I need not be afraid because You are, Immanuel, God with us, and the reign of Your Son Jesus will never end. You have the final victory!

Extra Space for Holy Spirit downloads and musings—use this space to journal and pray over anything God brings to your awareness.

Act Three

The Believing

"Mary asked the angel, 'How can this happen? I am a virgin.'

The angel replied, 'The Holy Spirit will come upon you, and the power of the Most high will overshadow you. So the baby to be born will be holy, and he will be called the Son of God. What's more, your relative Elizabeth has become pregnant in her old age! People used to say she was barren, but she has conceived a son and is now in her sixth month. For the Word of God will never fail.'

Mary **responded**, 'I am the Lord's servant. May everything you have said about me come true.' And then the angel left her."

(Luke 1:34-38 NLT)

The Journey Continues...

LISTEN

Listen to **Episode 39** of the **Kingdom Life Coaching Podcast** // *Untangled Advent //*
Act Three // The Believing.

Spotify

Apple

LOG

Jot down anything the Holy Spirit highlights to you throughout the teaching in this
episode.

_____

_____

_____

RECOGNIZE

Pay attention to what you're feeling. This brief section allows you the opportunity to **take stock of your worries** and give your concerns to God.

Write down a couple of specific things you'd like God to carry:

_____

_____

_____

_____

_____

RENEW

Cultivating an awareness of God's goodness is an excellent remedy for weariness. Identify three things you are grateful for today:

1.

2.

3.

Before you start reading the Scripture and journal questions, take a deep breath. Relax your heart and mind. Write a brief prayer of praise to God. Ask the Holy Spirit to meet you and speak to you throughout this study. Prepare yourself to hear from Him.

EXPLORE

Read the key Scripture passage for *Act Three //* **Luke 1:34-38**

- What is Mary's first very practical question regarding this impending pregnancy?

- What does Gabriel say in response to how this conception will happen?

- What does Mary learn about her cousin Elizabeth that might encourage her faith?

- Find **Luke 1:38** in your favorite Bible translation. Write Mary's resolute response of yielded faith below:

Related Scripture Readings for Further Exploration

What do you notice about the role belief (faith) plays in the experience of one's faith journey?

Acts 10:1-23 - Compare the story of Cornelius and Peter with that of Mary and Elizabeth. What do you notice about how God works between the connections of different people at the same time?

John 20:24-31 - What is Thomas' biggest challenge? What does Jesus say to him in verses 27 and 29?

Hebrews 11 - This chapter is often called the "hall of faith." Write down three names of people mentioned in this chapter and what they did to earn their place in this great legacy of faith. Who might you add to this list of people you know and why?

ASK:

Continue to go deep with your own thoughts and feelings. Journal your personal reflections below:

- The word "believe" means "to accept something as true, genuine, or real."[5] What is something God is inviting you to believe right now about His good plans and purposes - even and especially if you haven't seen or experienced them in the natural sense yet?

- One of my favorite little-known translations, The Voice, tells us Mary *"decided in her heart"* (Luke 1:38) to respond with assurance of faith to a seemingly impossible situation. Think of something about which you are anxious or worried. How can you lay this worry before Jesus right now? Write your prayer of surrender and belief below:

---

5   https://www.merriam-webster.com/dictionary/believe?src=search-dict-box

- I have a keen appreciation for the affectionately nicknamed apostle Doubting Thomas (see John 20:25). He simply wants to see the resurrected Jesus in order to believe such a thing truly happened! I soooo get that. In his mercy, Jesus reveals Himself to Thomas, but he also says, *"Blessed are those who haven't seen me and believe anyway"* (John 20:29 NLT). Guess what—this is you! You were not there to see the risen Christ, yet you believe. In what specific way is Jesus inviting you to grow in faith and trust with Him even if you don't see His hand at work in the natural sense?

- Mary's bold "yes" exposed her to immense personal risk. As an unwed mother, she would likely be shunned by her community and rejected by her fiancé, Joseph. And yet she responded, *"May everything you have said come true"* (Luke 1:38 NLT). What feels risky to you right now? How might God be preparing you to take a bold step of faith despite perceived personal risk and/or social consequences?

- One thing that might help shift your heart from doubt to belief is to testify of the things God has ALREADY done in your life! Life can be hard, crazy, unpredictable, and completely tangled up. And yet, God is still good! He is still on the throne. Write a prayer of thanksgiving for ways you have seen God's hand at work in spite of seemingly impossible circumstances:

Reflective Closing Prayer

Dear Lord, I admit there are times I don't walk in surrendered faith because I fear judgment or possible risk. Thank you that you see my doubts and love me despite my human failings. Even though I don't know how the future will turn out, I know you love me and constantly make all things new. I choose to yield myself, body and soul, to your plans and purposes because you are a gracious and loving Father who gives good gifts to your children.

Extra Space for Holy Spirit downloads and musings—use this space to journal and pray over anything God brings to your awareness.

_____

_____

_____

_____

_____

_____

_____

_____

_____

_____

_____

_____

_____

_____

_____

_____

_____

_____

Act Four

The Blessing

"A few days later Mary hurried to the hill country of Judea, to the town where Zechariah lived. She entered the house and greeted Elizabeth. At the sound of Mary's greeting, Elizabeth's child [John the Baptist] leaped within her, and Elizabeth was filled with the Holy Spirit.

Elizabeth gave a glad cry and exclaimed to Mary, 'God has **blessed** you above all women, and your child is **blessed**. Why am I so honored that the mother of my Lord should visit me? When I heard your greeting, the baby in my womb jumped for joy. You are **blessed** because you believed that the Lord would do what he said.'"

(Luke 1:39-45 NLT)

Digging Deeper...

LISTEN

Listen to **Episode 40** of the **Kingdom Life Coaching Podcast** // *Untangled Advent //*
Act Four // The Blessing.

Spotify

Apple

LOG

Jot down anything the Holy Spirit highlights to you throughout the teaching in this
episode.

_____

_____

_____

RECOGNIZE

This is likely a new day and you have new or lingering worries on your mind. Take a moment to cast your burdens on Jesus.

What would you like Him to carry for you today?

_____

_____

_____

_____

_____

RENEW

You are growing in your practice of thankfulness as a remedy for worry. Keep up the good work! Identify three things you are grateful for on this day:

1.

2.

3.

Before you start reading the Scripture and journal questions, take a deep breath. Relax your heart and mind. Write a brief prayer of praise to God. Ask the Holy Spirit to meet you and speak to you throughout this study. Prepare yourself to hear from Him.

EXPLORE

Read the key Scripture passage for *Act Four* // **Luke 1:39-45**

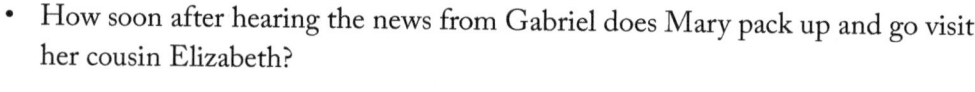

- How soon after hearing the news from Gabriel does Mary pack up and go visit her cousin Elizabeth?

- What happens to Elizabeth when Mary enters her home?

- As such, what is Elizabeth's greeting to Mary?

- Why does she call Mary "blessed"?

Related Scripture Readings for Further Exploration

Let's dig into the meaning of true spiritual blessing and how faith and obedience play a role in what we experience.

Matthew 5:1-12 - "Blessed are" literally means "happier are..." List three truths Jesus lays out in this Sermon on the Mount that resonate with you in this season.

Deuteronomy 28:1-10 - What is the connection between our obedience and many of the natural gifts of God?

Ephesians 1:1-14 - What (or who!) is the connection to our spiritual blessing? Why do we praise God, and for what do we praise Him?

Galatians 6:7-10 - It can often be tiring to "do good." But what does Paul tell us will happen if we don't give up?

ASK:

I pray this time of personal reflection and journaling has been enlightening and helpful! Keep it up, friend. Time spent in honest assessment is never wasted. God will honor your intentionality here!

- The word "blessed" in this passage comes from the Greek word "eulogeo" which means "favored of God, caused to prosper, or to make happy."[6] List a few of the specific blessings of mercy and grace God has bestowed on you in your lifetime.

- Read **Acts 11:21-23**. What does Barnabas observe when he gets to Antioch? As a result of this observation, what happens in Barnabas' heart, and what does he say to the believers there?

---

6   https://www.blueletterbible.org/nlt/luk/1/1/t_conc_974042

- God blessed Mary with confirmation of His capability for the miraculous when she heard about Elizabeth's pregnancy. As such, Mary headed out to visit her relative (vs. 39). Who has God put in your path as a wonderful encourager of your faith?

- Elizabeth rejoices when Mary shows up at her house. The baby in her womb (John the Baptist) immediately jumps for joy! She calls Mary *"blessed by God above all other women"* (Luke 1:42 NLT). Who could you write a note or send a text to as an encouragement to let them know you see God working in their life and rejoice with them in that call?

Reflective Closing Prayer

Dear Lord, Thank you that I never have to walk this journey of life alone. You are always with me and continually provide people to encourage me along the way. Help me to truly see these people and never take their love for granted. Open my eyes to see the ones you have prepared me to bless as well.

Extra Space for Holy Spirit downloads and musings—use this space to journal and pray over anything God brings to your awareness.

Act Five

The Rejoicing

"Mary responded,

'Oh, how my soul praises the Lord. How my spirit **rejoices** in God my Savior! For he took notice of his lowly servant girl, and from now on all generations will call me blessed.

For the Mighty One is holy, and he has done great things for me.

He shows mercy from generation to generation to all who fear him."

(Luke 1:46-50 NLT)

This is not the end, merely the beginning of continued encounter with God!

LISTEN

Listen to **Episode 41** of the **Kingdom Life Coaching Podcast** // *Untangled Advent // Act Four // The Rejoicing.*

Spotify

Apple

LOG

Jot down anything the Holy Spirit highlights to you throughout the teaching in this episode.

_____

_____

RECOGNIZE

How are you feeling right now?

Check-in with your thoughts and share anything with God that you want Him to untangle for you now:

_____

_____

_____

_____

_____

RENEW

You are nearing the end of this devotional journey! But not at all nearing the end of God's never-ending goodness. Praise Him for three good gifts He's already given you:

1.

2.

3.

Before you start reading the Scripture and journal questions, take a deep breath. Relax your heart and mind. Write a brief prayer of praise to God. Ask the Holy Spirit to meet you and speak to you throughout this study. Prepare yourself to hear from Him

EXPLORE

Read the key Scripture passage for *Act Five* // **Luke 1:46-56.** (The Magnificat)

- What does Mary offer as a response to this blessing?

- List all of the things Mary mentions regarding God's faithful character in this song of praise:

- What promise of God does she recognize in verses 54 and 55? What does this mean for the believers like you and me even today?

Related Scripture Readings for Further Exploration

Let's dig into the meaning of true spiritual blessing and how faith and obedience play a role in what we experience.

1 Samuel 2:1-10 - Hannah fervently prayed for a son and promised to dedicate him to the Lord's service. What observations stand out to you about her song in relation to Mary's?

Psalm 138 - List some of the declarations King David makes about God in his Psalm (response) of praise. Which ones remind you of Mary's reflections?

1 Peter 5:5-7 - What similarities do you find between Peter's exhortation and Mary's song? What posture or position are we as believers encouraged to take under the authority of our Holy God?

ASK:

These questions are your invitation to go deeper with Jesus and ask the Holy Spirit to help you access the innermost parts of your soul. I pray this time has been rich and will encourage you to keep journaling for a deeper understanding of yourself and God's work in your life!

- Mary's first response was one of praise. How can you respond in worship today as she did? Pull up the "Untangled Advent" Spotify playlist. Find a particular song* that speaks to your heart. Marinate in the music as an act of reverent worship to your King! Write down a couple of lyrics that specifically move your heart towards Him. (*If you need some guidance, "O What a King," by Katy Nichole is a beautiful song written from the perspective of what Mary might have been thinking.)

- How has God taken notice of you, as Mary suggests (Luke 1:48)? What legacy of faith do you want to leave future generations—especially around the holidays? What do you want to cultivate in your family? Write down your vision and prayer for generational legacy here.

- In order to live into and build that legacy, what feels important to you right now? Make a list of three core values you are currently exhibiting well and three things you sense the Lord inviting you to re-evaluate and possibly shift in some way in order to better align with your vision of a faith-filled legacy.

- What predominant perspective does Mary give us in her song? Over what areas of your life (or the world in general) do you need to trust God's sovereignty? What do you sense the Holy Spirit nudging you to let go of in order to be fully submitted to the Lord and His will?

- The classic Christmas hymn, "O Holy Night," reminds us Jesus' arrival brought long-awaited hope to a weary world. And His resurrection brings supernatural joy and eternal life to our souls. As this study comes to a close, what feels important to you right now? Write out a prayer of thanksgiving for all the Lord revealed to you over these past weeks, spending time with Him and in His Word. *What do you want to carry with you into Christmas and beyond in order to live in the peace and freedom only Jesus can bring?*

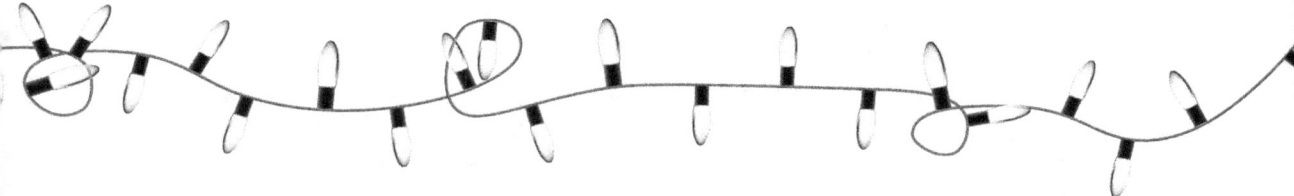

Reflective Closing Prayer

Dear Lord, When I reflect on all you have done for me, my heart is overwhelmed with gratitude. You are truly the One and only King! I come to you with all that I am. I lay my tender burdens at your feet. Thank you for the peace you offer in the midst of chaos and the joy available to me in the darkest of nights. I am forever and always—yours.

Extra Space for Holy Spirit downloads and musings—use this space to journal and pray over anything God brings to your awareness.

Denouement

- or as I would say - Wrapping it Up!

Biblical historians tell us there were 400 years of "silence" between the words penned in the Old Testament and the New Testament's first words. There are no recorded or archived prophecies or letters available to us from this time period. Does this silence imply that God was absent? That He chose not to speak or intervene? That He had forgotten His people?

The truth is we don't know the answer to this question regarding the details of life on Earth at that time, but we do know God's sovereign, faithful, unchanging character of justice, grace, and love for His people. And even in the bleakest of spaces, He was preparing to send the Light who would come and dwell among us and reconcile His children to Himself. This Light would illuminate the darkest of nights and profoundly transform the course of human history forever.

It's likely your life isn't neatly packaged or tied up with a bow, even after completing this study. There may still be situations or circumstances that feel uncertain, strained, and weary. You might wonder if God notices your confusion and pain. The short answer is YES! He sees you and He cares. Jesus came into the world as a physical representation of God's unconditional, ever-present, transformative love.

Jesus is the free gift of hope for all who believe. And if you willingly receive this gift, the Light of the world now lives in YOU through the power and presence of the Holy Spirit! You can go from here trusting His Light will minister to you, and will shine through you as a beacon of hope to a weary world.

I pray your exploration and examination of God's Word throughout this study has reminded you of God's incredible grace, and Mary's obedient, surrendered faith inspires you to keep expecting hope and looking for the Light.

The book of Lamentations shares a profound truth you can tuck in your heart all year long as a reminder of God's continual Light, hope, and love—on even the *silentest* of nights:

"The faithful love of the LORD never ends!
His mercies never cease.
Great is his faithfulness;
His mercies begin afresh each morning.
I say to myself, 'The LORD is my inheritance; therefore, I will hope in
him!'"

(Lamentations 3:22-24 NLT)

Prayers. Key Takeaways.
And Other Holy Spirit
Inspired Musings....

About the Author

*M*egan Nilsen is the author of the *Untangled Faith book and journal*, which guides readers to discern the voice of God for themselves and learn to glean Kingdom wisdom through the beautiful exchange journaling method. She hosts the popular Kingdom Life Coaching podcast and works as a Kingdom clarity coach, empowering people of all ages to listen to God's voice in order to achieve the exciting plans and purposes He has for them! She is a sought–after retreat speaker and lives in Colorado. Megan and her husband enjoy exploring newfound freedom in the (almost) empty-nester life and hopping on a plane as often as possible to visit their young adult children.

If you want to know more about their international adoption story and God's transformative, healing work in Megan's heart, you can read about it all in her first book, *A Beautiful Exchange: Responding to God's Invitation for More.*

One favor to ask: If you have liked any of Megan's books, including this one, please go to Amazon to leave a review! This will help others find and trust these important resources as well. Thank you!

Website: meganbnilsen.com

Podcast: Kingdom Life Coaching

Instagram: @megan_nilsen

Facebook: Megan Bradley Nilsen

Other Titles
by Megan Nilsen

A Beautiful Exchange

Megan's journey leads her to discover the
Kingdom of God and live her true identity,
demonstrating that God's highest calling is
the same for everyone.

Untangled Faith

How Honest Conversations
with God Lead to Deeper Connections,
Clarity, and Peace

Untangled Faith
A Beautiful Exchange Journal